T0077977

BLESS YOU

BRANDON JACKSON

authorHOUSE

AuthorHouse™
1663 Liberty Drive
Bloomington, IN 47403
www.authorhouse.com
Phone: 833-262-8899

© 2020 Brandon Jackson. All rights reserved.

No part of this book may be reproduced, stored in a retrieval system, or transmitted by any means without the written permission of the author.

Published by AuthorHouse 09/28/2020

ISBN: 978-1-7283-6189-5 (sc)
ISBN: 978-1-7283-6190-1 (hc)
ISBN: 978-1-7283-6188-8 (e)

Print information available on the last page.

Any people depicted in stock imagery provided by Getty Images are models, and such images are being used for illustrative purposes only. Certain stock imagery © Getty Images.

This book is printed on acid-free paper.

Because of the dynamic nature of the Internet, any web addresses or links contained in this book may have changed since publication and may no longer be valid. The views expressed in this work are solely those of the author and do not necessarily reflect the views of the publisher, and the publisher hereby disclaims any responsibility for them.

dou·ble en·ten·dre

/ˌdo͞obl än'tändrə,ˌdəbl än'tändrə/

noun

1. a word or phrase open to two interpretations, one of which is usually risqué or indecent.

    "he was unable to get through two consecutive sentences without a smutty double entendre"

Senryū

Form of poetry

Description

Senryū is a Japanese form of short poetry similar to haiku in construction: three lines with 17 morae. Senryū tend to be about human foibles while haiku tend to be about nature, and senryū are often cynical or darkly humorous while haiku are more serious.

Special Thank you...

I would like to thank, Mom, Cindy Jackson, Brother, Kalan Jackson for helping with the editing and friend Maria for pushing the boulder up the hill.

For that Thank You!

There are three books inside this book.

This book is Dedicate to my son. In this book, there are some truths and some not so true it is up to you the reader to decide which is which.

With big eyes
Poked out lip,
But, but Daddy...
Toddler Trickery

Bowing out
She would end
Her day prayers and night ones too with Amen,
So GOD
Placed me a man in her path Pause...
I've run the tread out my max's, usually, I don't accept failure,
however, I'm done.
It's not fair to want you more then you want me sooo this is me
gracefully...bowing out.

Confused, so..
No legs, no feet
But you are a...
Sneakerhead

Clean apartment,
Scented candles lit...
Doorbell...
Lies and Deceptions

She pushed
And I pulled,
The moral is a cover thief.
First Sleepover

He feels
Midnight blue,
Not your typical......
Breakup

True love
Or is it just like,
Riddle me this.
Magic 8 ball

He tells the
Best stories,
B.T.W he's....
Only 3 and 3 quarters

Trees are greener
The sunlight
So bright
Born Blind

Gym shorts
Tank top and sneakers
Streetball.
Driveway dreams

Cross over
Pivot foot grounded,
Pull back
Fadeaway

First Date

The scarlet red dress hugged her figure 8 shape, she strolled over to the table, no fable all eyes were on her shimmy, him and her. Clearly, the perfume complimented her.

Her essence was off the pages I was hooked on her Cloe it molested my nose. No, I wasn't offended pulling out her chair as I started looking for paint strokes.

She slowly sipped her rum and coke, waiter I'm ready to order fell off her lips. I'll have the shrimp salad and dressing on the side and you sir?

The Same.

I used to run
Walk freely,
Now I roll
Life (with MS)

I have remembered
Way more things than I thought
I have forgotten.
Lost and Found

A Slam Poets Saga
I was asked why do Slam poets yell? Well, it's to drive home a point, point being I Am Adamant. Passionate about my topic. So your privileged ass, really great school district, with a gated community... Needs to stop it!
You couldn't walk a mile in my kicks, we choose the less problematic route to arrive alive, we have a low attendance rate cause today won't be the day my Momma gets called saying "Ma'am there's been an accident with your son."
So stop trying to procreate my struggle, it's real – REAL TALK. This is why I yell, so you feel me.. **YOU FEEL ME.**

I thought
December was cold,
Then she walks in
Coldest Woman Ever (CWE)
She's cute, pretty even!
Too bad,
She reached her peak
Junior High Hottie

If You Are Available

Let's just say you don't have a man and was thinking you'd like a counterpart, wait... Hi, I am your first and last kiss.

If we slept together, we'd be that couple, friends would talk about us behind our backs.

Our story would be in Oprah's book club or even on New York's best sellers list, but only if you are available.

Hi-hat, Kick
Middle row on keys,
No bass
2 Man Band

Let's race.
Bet I beat you to the lights.
OK, GO!
Street Lights (6:59 pm)

Slow Jamz.
Lights turned low.
Soo...
Mr. Nasty Time
While mid-conversation,
she sneezed. Causing me to sneeze.
I said, "Bless you,"

Ditto

He was Mr. Steal
Your girl sharp.
His credit was not.
She couldn't tell.

One Hundred

HA CHU, HA CHU
Pause REALLY
Nobody will say it
Bless you (Thank You)
Bless You

Flag on the Play

She threw red flags like a south-central PIRU, and I knew I knew she would be wrong.. But those rose-colored lenses played a part and standing too close to the tree I missed her forest of lies; however, self-ignorance was bliss. I thought

we'd gladly wrap this issue. "See, this is why I'm done," she said. "But umm.. Baby, boo," He said, "Since this isn't going in my favor Imma step out." "GET OUT!" she screamed. So I left.

She only sees
The good in him,
No his red flags or previous ways.

Love Blinders

Do you remember
My EX bae Rebecca?
You know her now as Becky.

Eskimo Brothers

Peanut Love

She asked me, "Is it a crime to find myself lost in the rapture?" When
I sigh I give her cardiac arrest, a test of will power.

She told me, I power walk through her thoughts.

She also said she wanted to avoid me, stay home "sick" but, it's not
that simple.

"He be calling me", she said, Like Pookie. I'll be your Woodstock only
if you'd be my....Snoopy."

So quick question,
Since you still frock the carat
Are you taken or not?
Mrs. or Miss

Real Talk
I would like to say first....I'm sorry, I was wrong. So to you, I'm sorry.
I don't say that much but yeah, I chose wrong, no song. You can
blame it all on me.
Like poor visibility on the highway, I missed my exit... my turn...
lesson learned.
Look I am nuts for you. True, I want to rebuild what we had. Same
plot, different studs. Love is the makeup, Cover girl. I want you.
Please don't let my wants supersede my need to have you back. Now
That's....Real Talk.

I want to tell you I like you,
Like you!
But that's as far as it can go....
Deep Feelings

I woke up fiending.
Got those mid-morning jitters,
but no coffee cup.
Bugga Sugga

Elmar Love
I inhale her, Exhale the thought of us parting. Ahh hell, I found myself lost in another one. Once again. Hopefully, like gorilla glue mixed with superglue...nothing can cause us to fade away.

She Had Me At Hello
She puts the Spring in my step like March, April, May! I asked, are you happy with ya last name? Cause I'd change mine. I'd be Mr. Brandon R. whatever your last name is. I'm told it's Progressive or is it Allstate? At any rate me as ya man, babe, you're in good hands.

I dreamed about a
Waterfall...My faucet leaks,
Wait....I gotta pee.
Wet Dreams

Just because we lip locked
and held hands that means
we go together now?
Technicalities

She saw him out
With her but didn't react.
So how was your day boo?
Playing it Coy

I do not think she's
Pregnant for real,
But she got elastic pants on.
Sorry not Sorry

She finds her solace in cigarettes
throughout the day,
but no in me.
Square Root

So since her lips
Are chapped.
All I can give her are
Eskimo kisses.
Rough Smooches

He told me that white milk
tasted better than chocolate milk.
He's false.
Racist Much?

He is too young
To grasp the concept
that he is naked yet.
Just free.
To be innocent

He reminds me
That we had
Sex at least one time
During our marriage.
My Seed

Soooo, question...
Are you leaving
me for my friend?
He replied, "Yes, I am."
Informal 2-week notice

She was kind of a
Redbone, good teeth,
Nice ASSets, but them eyebrows though.....
Freda Kahlo

Mom used to push me ion the swing.
Dad pushed me in the pool but no more.
Now....
Electric Wheelchair

My wife shops and
Runs up the credit bill.
I wait to see the results.
Husband Duties
Granddad wore a
Navy suit, floral top too
with the red gator boots.
Miami Pimpin

Girls night out.
Four shots in
Lemon drop martinis
And she left with him.
Plan B Pill

Lavender skies
Magenta clouds,
Raspberry trees
Grapevines
Acid
70 Something

"I want to pet that kitty."
"I want to hold that cat."
"My cat"?
Free Kitten

She is gorgeous on
The outside, but her
Insides though are not so much.
Pretty Ugly***

She gave a weak notice
To her boss that she
Was leaving in a week.
Sick of Being Sick

I could feel the wind zipping
Past my facial hair as
I went down aisle 8.
Grocery Store Electric Cart

I buy retro Jordans now
Because I couldn't afford
It back then.
Retribution

My lady pushes
Me uphill
Without any help.
Now that's real love.
Heuristic

I am not saying it did not happen,
I just do not recall it.
One Too Many

The heat index
was 98 degrees,
Her breath was kinda hot too.
Close Talker

I got a ticket,
Cross the lane,
Moving too fast.
Didn't see the ground.
DWI (In a wheelchair)

A long kiss goodnight
Potentially leads to us
Having a cup of....
Coffee in the Morning

Riddle me this pervert
What ya looking at?
Got something on your chest?
Titty Sweat

"No questions asked," She said.
As she got in the car, "I am O.T. Dub."
P.I.C (Partner In Crime

She was reluctant to take
Her top off because of
What I may think.
National Geographic Titties

She doesn't have 20/20 vision.
She is visually impaired.
Glasses Freak

He said with big eyes,
"I love you!"
She responded,
"I like you too friend".
Miscommunication

Douglas said that he will only
Get naked in a
Pitch black bedroom.
No Bright Ideas

My wife tried to convince me,
Travel sex was better
then at home sex.
Same OLD Same

My little cousin DJ
LOVES his
Alone time,
Long STEAMY shower.
Finding Out What It Does

There's a small list of things
You should never ever say
To your lady
Getting a Little Hippy

She pulled me close
So you know what that means,
Mr. Nasty time.
Girl stop.
Adult Horse Play

I am very confused.
Soo, you not but you
Just look it in those pants.
S.N.S (Sorry Not Sorry) 2

BINGO!, That's my car
NO, WAIT,
That IS my car.
BINGO

I'm sure
I more than likely hid my Radio
Face again.
My AAA card couldn't fit in these
super skinny jeans.
My First Car

I had a cheat dream,
woke up in a cold sweat.
Texted her my deepest sorry.
Real Love

Momma Bear is Sick
I hope I say aloud
Get better sooner rather than later
I have plans for us.

Sad to say but my beautiful mother is
Confined to a hazmat bubble.
When she felt better, I gave her the biggest
airport kind of hug!

USIE Time you say?
Hey, Daddy, he said,
I have a brilliant idea
What if together we went
Upstairs as a pair and watch a few
Of my favorite TV shows.

I have been told
To put the lotions
Back in the bucket every time.
Do As You're Told

She is walking around
Top-less as if she is
saying do you like?
S4L (Sisterhood For Life)

"Excuse me,
You two ladies, " He said,
"May I buy one of you a drink"?
First Come First Serve

"Do me a favor" ...
"Anything for you", I said.
"Drop ya pants and cough".
Prostate Exam

You are doing it the
wrong way honey bun
A breast exam's like this.
Breast Exam

"We have to get checked
boo thang," he said.
"Heads or Tails, let's see who goes first."
NEW RELATIONSHIP

Clenched tight butt cheeks.
I got home and killed a bottle of
Pepto Bismol.
Homemade Colonic

Can't help the fact that I love spicy foods. The spicier the better.
Ghost Pepper Tacos

NEED TO KNOW BASIS
"Say, babe," she said, "My absolute favorite ice cream is Dutch
Chocolate."
She says, "Let's get a cone
2 scoops of MY fav."
Then she asks, "You like it tho right?"
All this time she never asked what's your flavor?

Animal Love
Her snoring sounds like
A bear stuck in a paper sack until I roll her.

Her naked body under sheets makes up for teeth grinding at about
3 AM.

Snuggles like a wolverine just as vicious in lite sleep.

HAIR TODAY GONE TOMORROW
It took 5 years to grow but just under an hour to cut my hair.
I started it for her but it was my decision to let them go again.
Wanted to donate the hair yet no takers. Now the line is wrapped
around the block.

Fireflies
My MRI was like a jar of fireflies Doc said those were Plaques.
I didn't get the gist of MS, I just knew I had limits, a self-timer.

BESHIER HALL
In the den with the lights out watching a scary flick
and a shadow moved.

Went to investigate to prove I'm no punk; however, It was a
black car.

Had no animals, I shot a rubber band and he hissed. Now we have
a cat.

Sleeping Bag

He's the friend you need
In a clinch, not a lot of questions, ride or die.

Met on a whim
Instantly knew he was the homie, despite his high school.

He was kicked out of his parent's house and stayed with me in
a....sleeping bag

Debate Fighter

You know, hands down I would fight for you, go to war too, but with
words though.

Clandestine

Remember that one time we said
we'd never tell
but you let it slip?

Is this still good

Raid my fridge with questions peeling back
Tupperware, bro is this still good?

The Good, Bad and Ugly of Marriage

Met her, liked her, and she did too.
Dated, marriage class, 7 years is a good start.
Now, I thought this would be blissful.
A kid changes a lot....
She slid me a piece of paper and said,
"Sign here..." Ending

Intro / Outro

This book is dedicated to pain, heartbreak, and anguish....you caused them, so I wrote them.

Modern-day witchcraft (Her)
Tried voodoo to keep him to no avail, guess chicken feet won't work.

MOVING BUSHES
I wonder if he can see me see him hiding in those bushes.

Bust It Wide Open
He can never know you wanna play some music?
Got this mix he made.

<u>Modern-day Witchcraft (Him)</u>
I guess she could see me watching her comings and goings.
Moving bushes

He came home to the same song playing loudly whenever, he would make love.
Bust it wide open.

Mr. Big talk, swear he can last long.
That is what he told me, he lied.
3 Pumps GO

Quick Draw
He has four kids with two possible.
So he asked her, "Do you judge much"?

Poison
I hate it.
But I told you
About her only
Because you asked me.

Hug Life
Could you put an orange Care bear standing with its arms out on my neck, please?

Naked Wrestling
Kid's asleep
Washing machine on the spin cycle.
Me and the Mrs....Naked Wrestling.

The Haunting
Let me find out
You moved on
Before I died....
You will feel my presence.

No kisses for you daddy
I asked my son for a hug goodnight.
As I leaned in, he told me...
Ummm...
No kisses for you daddy.

Que the Sax
Our kids are at the Grandparents house for the weekend. Go ahead and Que the SAX.

Hungry Much
My brothers come over and raid the fridge. Then they ask is this still good?

Our Day
I looked over at
My son, you are here.
He said, "Today is our day"...

Parent-Teacher Conference
Sooo, let me get this right...
This is an in-person meeting, I need pants?

Food Truck Friday
Food truck lines are
Like Jordan release dates.
You have to get there early.

OTTA BABY IT'S A BOY
She said she is positive it is positive.
Plus sigh means this time.
Otta baby it's a boy.

6-Floor Walk-up (Grocery Day)
The elevator works some times and some times it doesn't. Take the stairs....6-floor walk.

WE fuss, We fight
But I'm the one who has to sleep on the couch at night.
So Not Fair

Looking in the mirror,
I was feeling myself
Like I lost my keys.
Blind Date

Kim, I know we haven't talked in 3 weeks but wanna go on a date?
3 Dots (iPhone 6S)

My best friend died.
My only duty
is to clear his search
history.
Computer Love

My son can't read yet, but he always reads me like an open book.
3   y/o B.F.F

Do you remember that one time I came through to help you move
that couch
Guilt-Tripping

She picked out our therapist. Stretched out to the limit, stressed out.
Let's Talk
Couples Therapy

Just Let Them Be

I, myself, am an extravert she is an introvert, but we make it work.
So I know
she needs her space; I won't bother her till she shows her face.
It's important to know your counterpart, it starts with a simple
convo and understanding.
When she gets home, she needs to decompress. No stress, no ill
feelings are thrown my way. She just needs to ready her mind for
round two it's not me boo.

Uber D

She asked me to give her that dot, dot, dot...
That chickenpox itch, you know the one you can't scratch. So, like
Dim Sum, she called in her some Uber D.

Crushing

See I watch her lost in like. I like you, like I like....Like you. I hope I
don't have to like you from afar....So I hope the feeling is mutual.

Creeper

A mere convo can cause a cardiac arrest. Side note: I can follow you on IG but don't let me follow you in real life.

I'm called a stalker any way... I mean yeah, I've been caught crouching outside bushes but that is not the point. I try to stay out of pointing sight.

#ME Too

She was on the me-too before it grew legs. She'd be leaving the bedroom headed for work, I would say love you babe. Her response would be me too.

Her kisses felt obligated not like when we dated. She checked out but blamed me for the twin size distance in our Cali King.

They say distance makes your heart grow closer, nope. #metoo.

The Calm before the storm

One would assume, I excel in ballet the way I moved so gracefully and elegantly over eggshells. If one broke all hell would break loose.

Liar

She's a lion not just lying down. She said she would be down in sickness health or wealth.

Conclusion

To God, you lied so to him you must answer. I love the fact you birthed my seed. We had a union at one point but now that's over and I'm done.

Printed in the United States
By Bookmasters

Printed in the United States
By Bookmasters